A Note to Parents and Teachers

The activites in this project book are designed to accompany the first grade text, Gift of Life, of the *...and these thy gifts* religious education series. When used in this way this Project Book serves as an extension of the program, assisting children in the development of a number of important learning and participatory skills.

These activites may also be used as a separate program of review and reinforcement for children using any basal religious education program. All the information needed to complete each page or section is provided in the book.

A very important aspect of the type of activities and projects suggested in this book is adult interest and reinforcement. Children should not look upon the completion of activities as "busy work" or homework, but rather as an opportunity to reflect on the classroom or home experience where the concepts dealt with were first learned or discussed. As reflections, the outcomes of the projects are meant to be shared with others.

The ideal method to use with this book is to first explain the activity to the child, then encourage the child to complete the activity, and finally share his or her ideas and reflections with others, parents, children, teacher.

We suggest that the activities not be graded, but discussed. One child's artwork or ideas should not be compared with those of other children, but rather combined with the work of the entire group to produce an overall view of the ideas and responses of the entire class. Each child is to be praised for his or her efforts, and encouraged to contribute creatively to the group's understanding of the themes presented by the program.

The Name Game

Write your name in the star or sunburst.

Ask your teacher or a friend to help you cut out your name-tag. You can make a poster with the name-tags of all the children in your group, or all the people in your family.

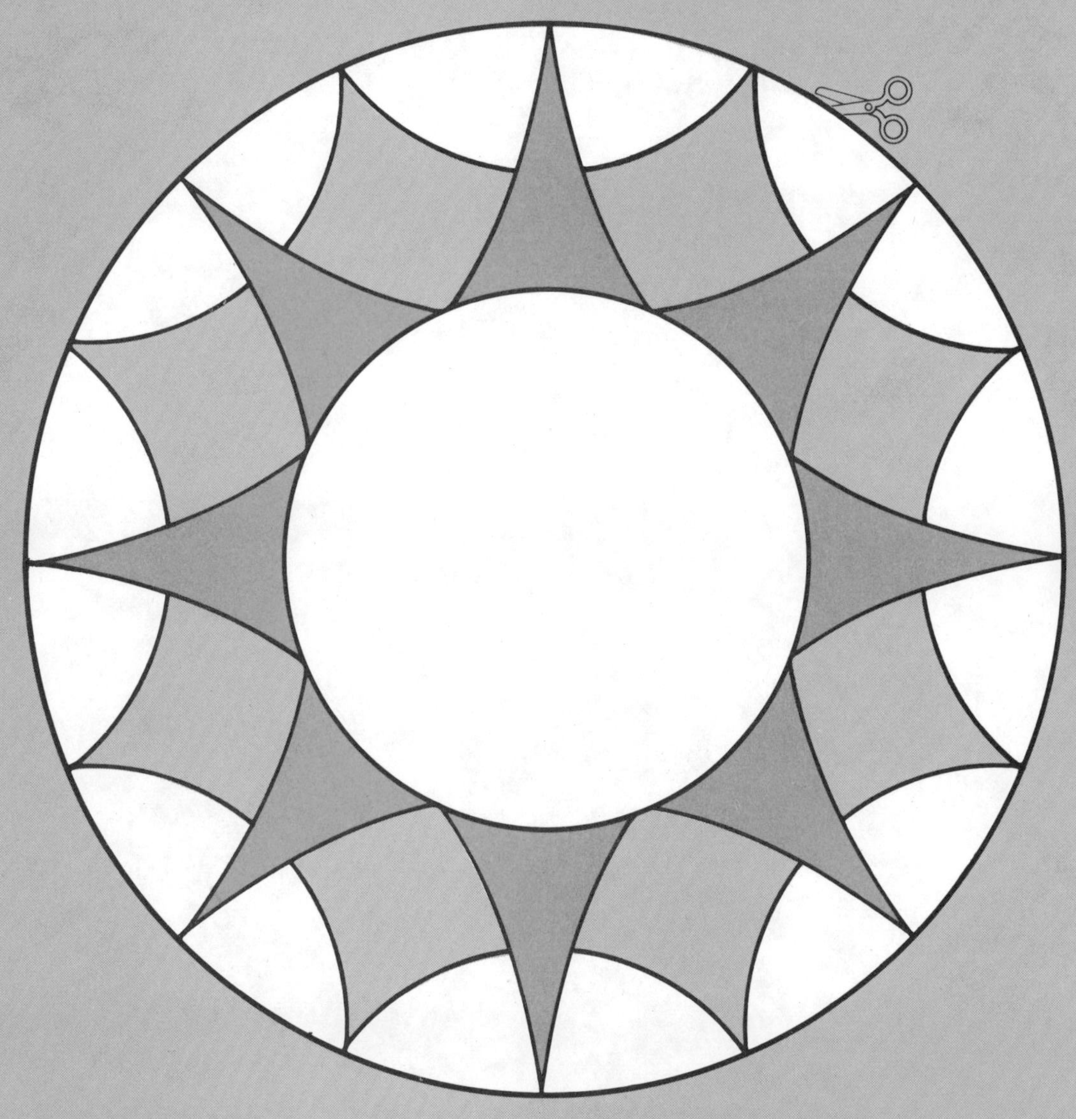

Can you find the hidden name?

Color in the spaces with crayons or felt-tip markers.

Use red for spaces marked **1**.

Use blue for spaces marked **2**.

Use green for spaces marked **3**.

Use yellow for spaces marked **4**.

God loves me!

My name is

This is what I look like. God loves me because I
am me.

My Gift Box

Follow the directions for making your **gift box.** Your teacher, or a parent, or a friend can help you put it together.

Cut on the solid lines: _________

Fold on the broken lines: _ _ _ _ _

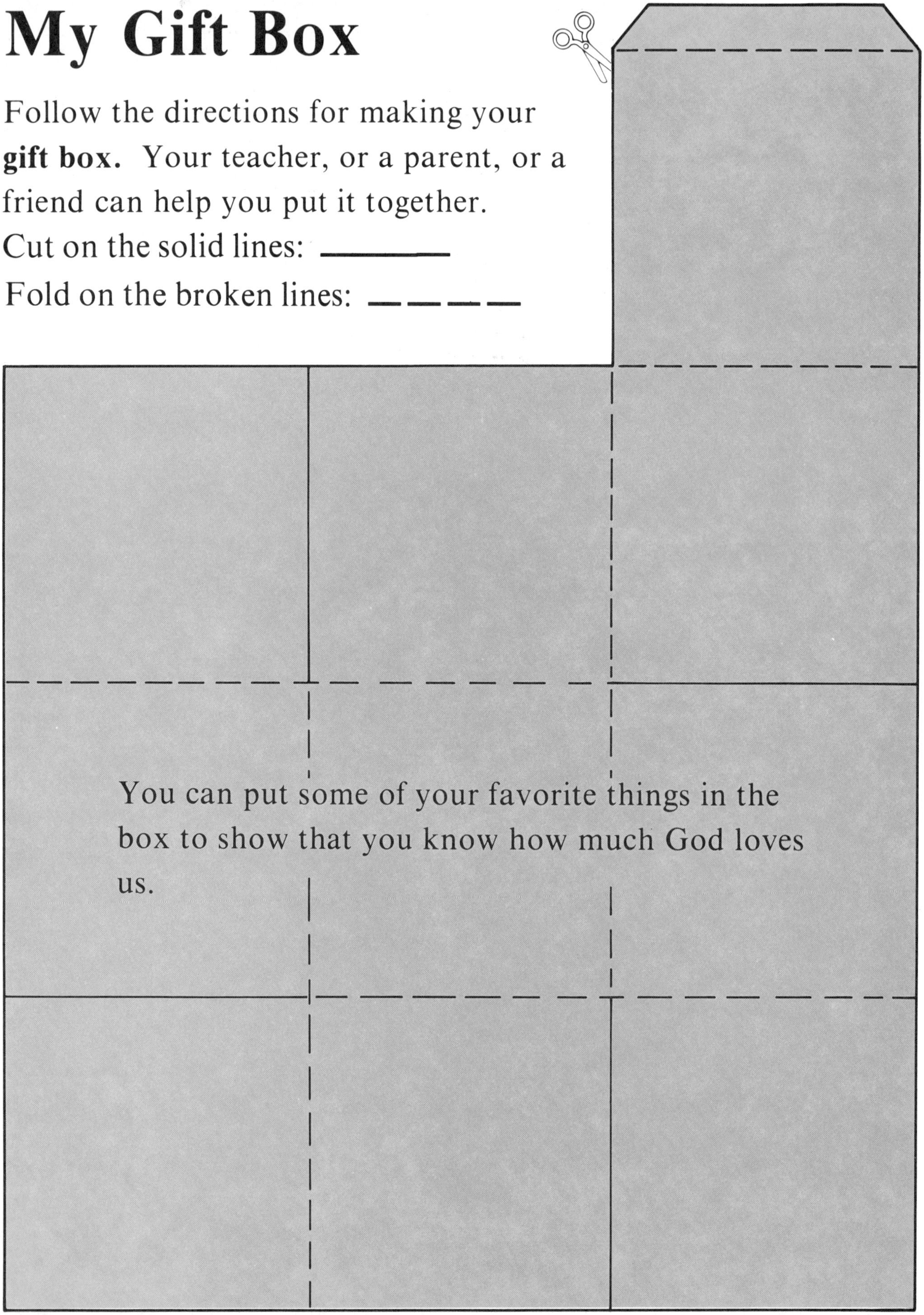

You can put some of your favorite things in the box to show that you know how much God loves us.

I
LOVE
GOD
AND
ALL
HIS
GIFTS

Creation — God's Gifts to Us

I know the things God created.

Color each picture. Cut out the pictures and
paste them on a sheet of paper to make a "picture
of creation." Paste the names beside each
picture, too.

dog   **cat**   **flower**   **horse**

Hidden-Picture Page

(God-made things)

Hidden-Picture Page

(Man-made things)

More of God's Gifts

Write an 'X' on the things that God gave people
the ability to make. Color the things that only
God can make.

God Our Father

I will trace the dots to know the word.

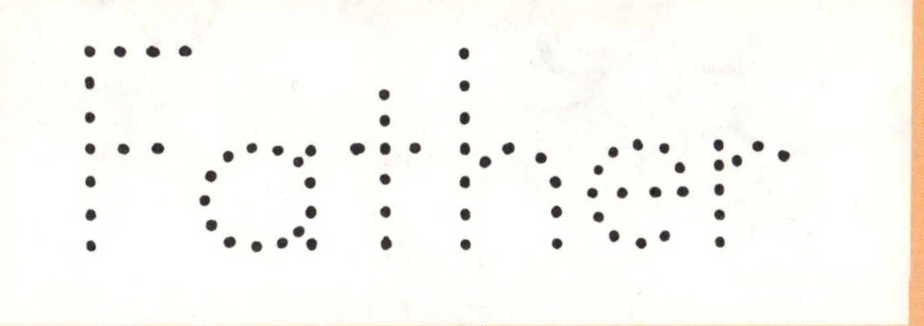

Cut out the puzzle pieces and fit them to make the word FATHER.

A Prayer

Our Father in
heaven, your
name is holy.

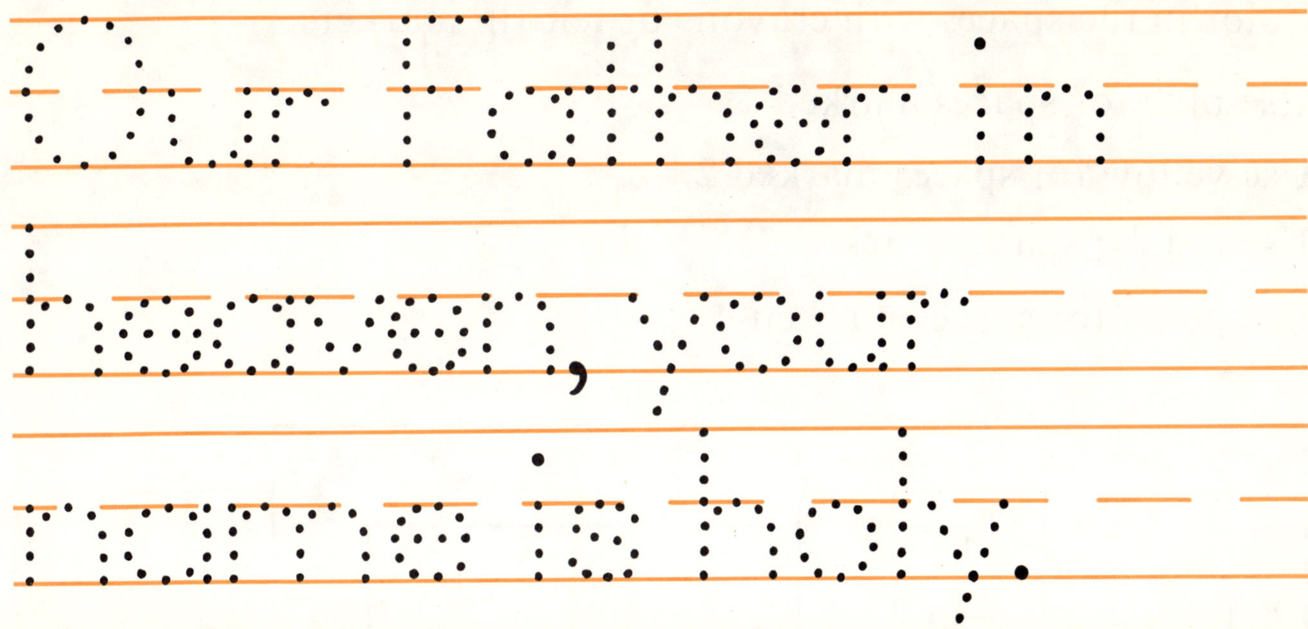

My Picture of God in Heaven

Can you find the hidden name?

Color in the spaces with crayons or felt-tip markers.

Use blue for spaces marked **1**.

Use yellow for spaces marked **2**.

Use red for spaces marked **3**.

Use green for spaces marked **4**.

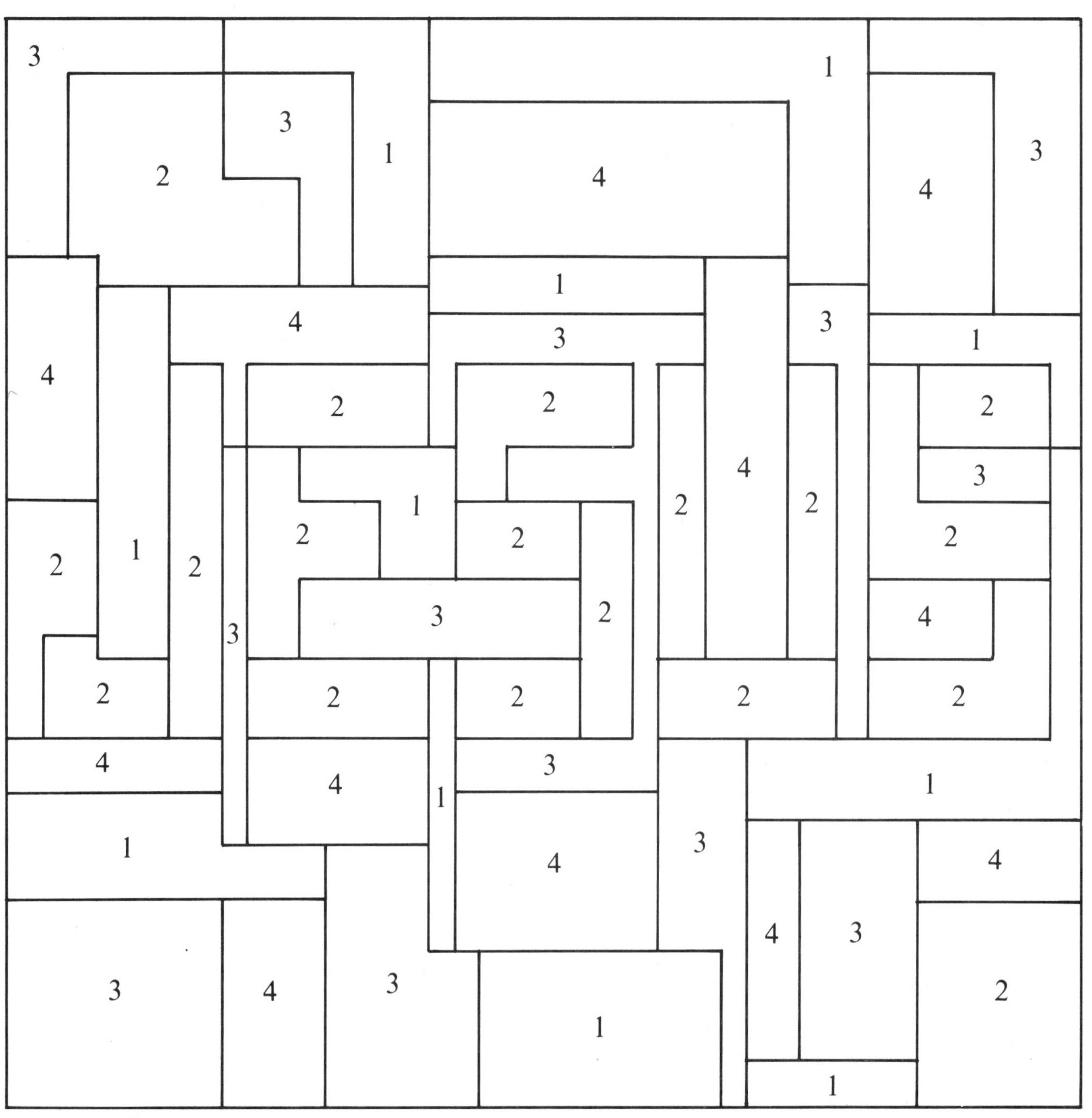

Gifts of the Father

I will draw the special Gifts of the Father to me.

My favorite pet or animal.

People who love me.

God's Creation

I will make a place for each of these creatures to live happily.

I love God's creation and will care for it.

Find the things that need to be taken away from the park to make it beautiful. Cross those things out with a pencil or dark-color crayon.

What can I do to keep these living things alive and as beautiful as God wishes them to be?

My Family Circle

These are pictures of members of my family:

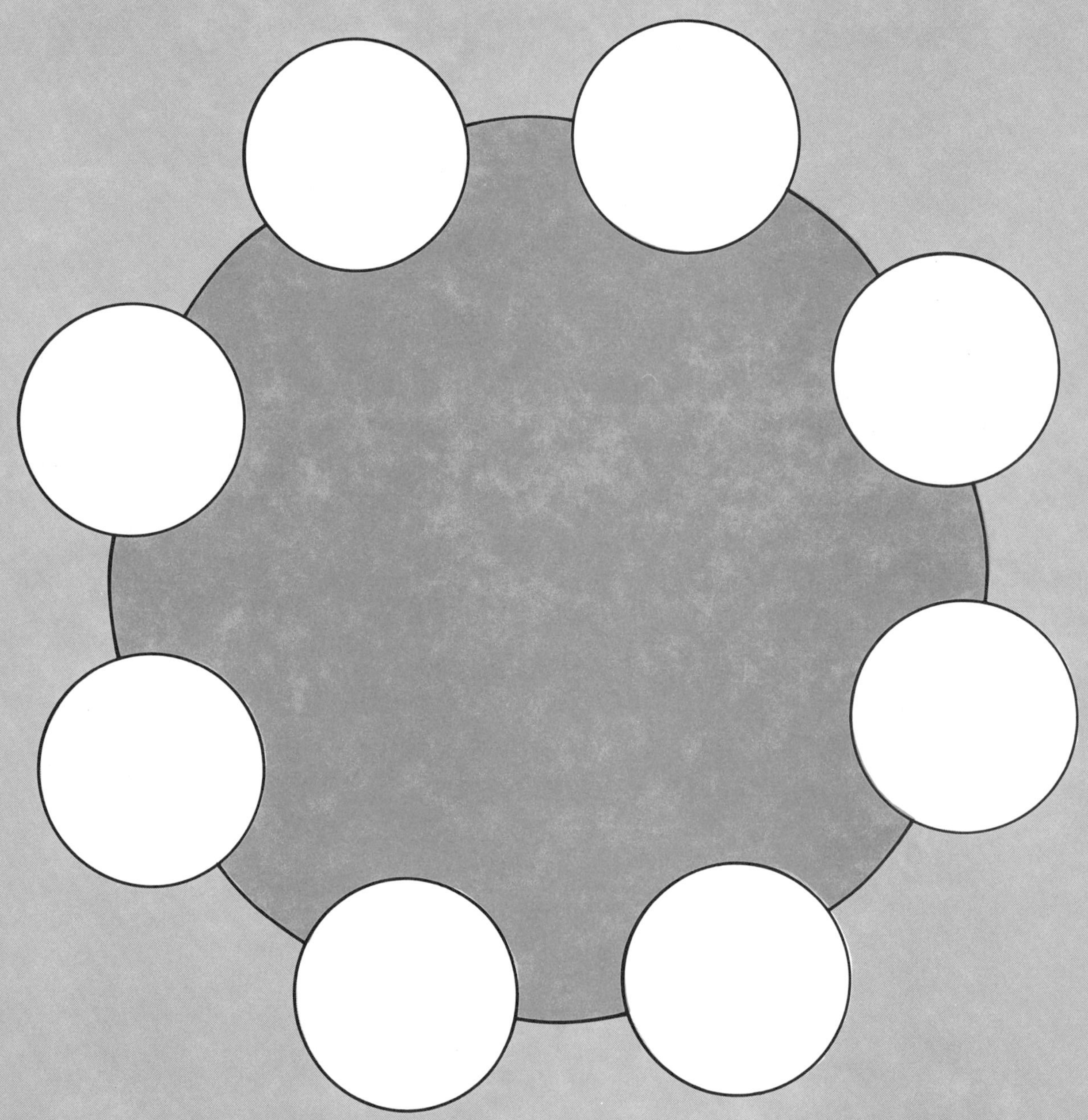

My last name

The Good News

Unscramble these words and write what Jesus said:

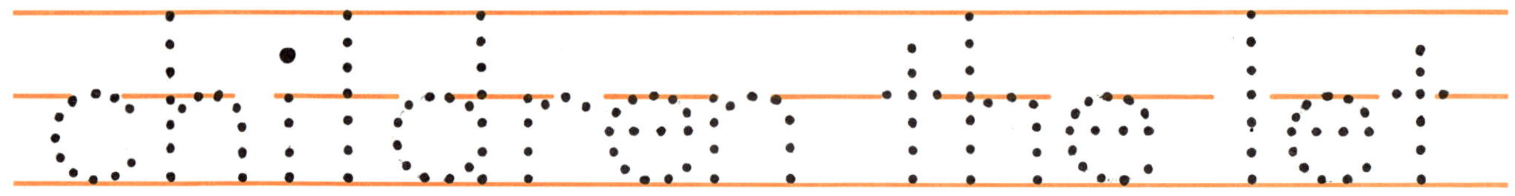

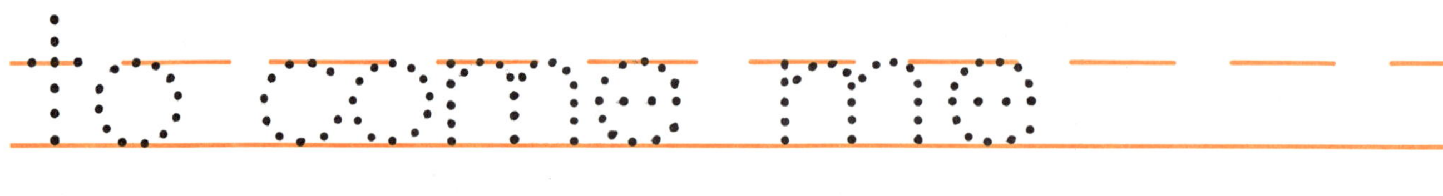

Can you find the hidden name?

Color in the spaces with crayons or felt-tip
markers. Try these colors, or choose other colors.
Use green for spaces marked **1**.
Use red for spaces marked **2**.
Use orange for spaces marked **3**.
Use brown for spaces marked **4**.

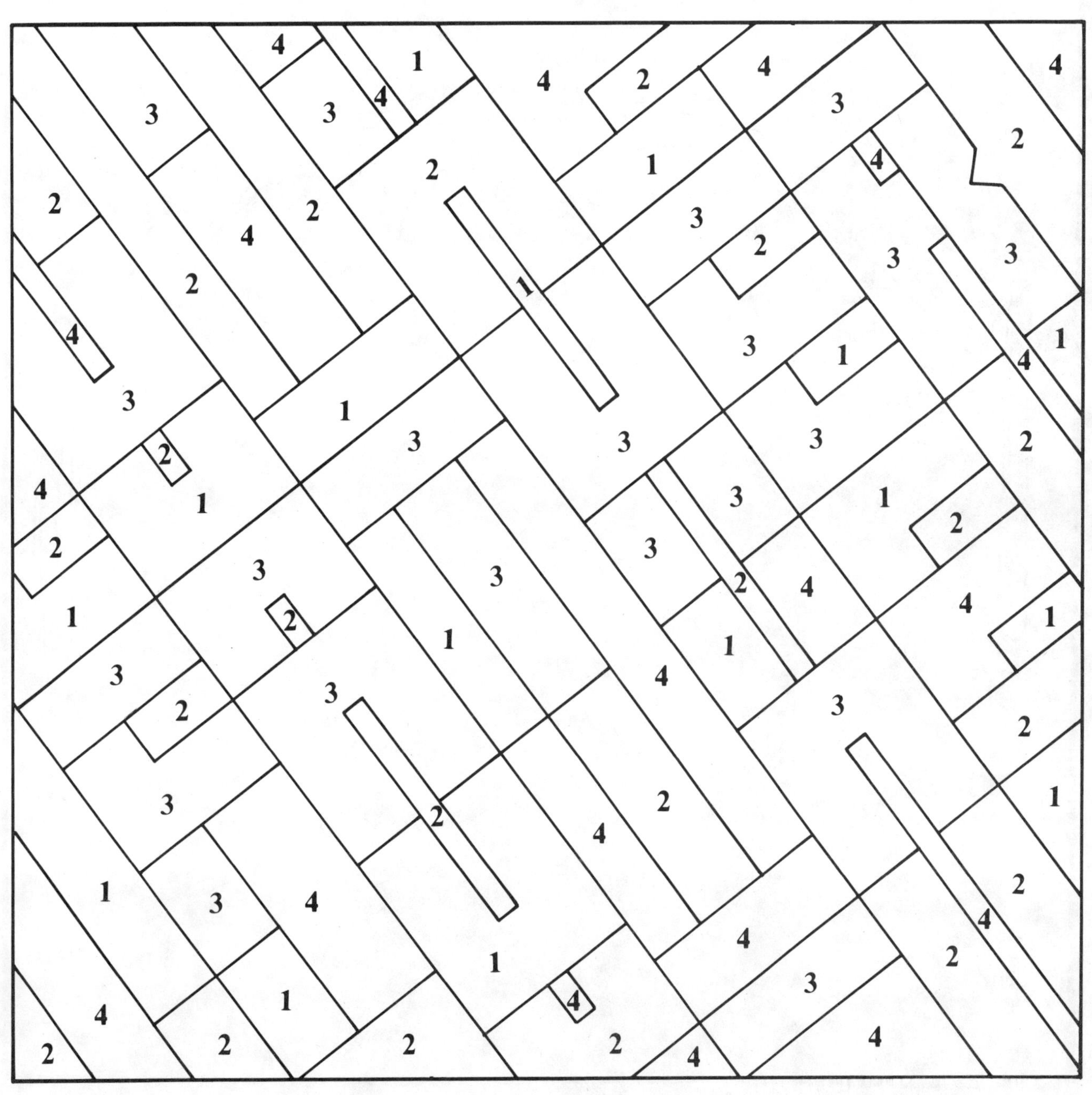

The Good Shepherd calls each sheep by name.

Draw the Good Shepherd and his sheep.

I have called you by name.

When I was baptized, I was named

CERTIFICATE OF BAPTISM

Church:_______________________________

This is to certify

That _______________________________

Child of _______________________________

and _______________________________

born in _______________________________

the _______ day of _______ , 19 ___ , was Baptized

on the _______________ day of _______ , 19 ___

According to the Rite of the
Roman Catholic Church

by the Rev. _______________________________

the Sponsors being _______________________

and _______________________________

as appears from the Baptismal Register of this Church.

Dated _______________

Pastor _______________

God's family comes together in church.

My parish church looks like this:

My parish church looks like this:

These are some of the people I see in church:

The Lost Sheep

Where could a sheep be lost? Draw in the lost sheep
in this picture. Color the picture.

Connect the dots to find something shepherds use to
help them look after their sheep. Color the
picture.

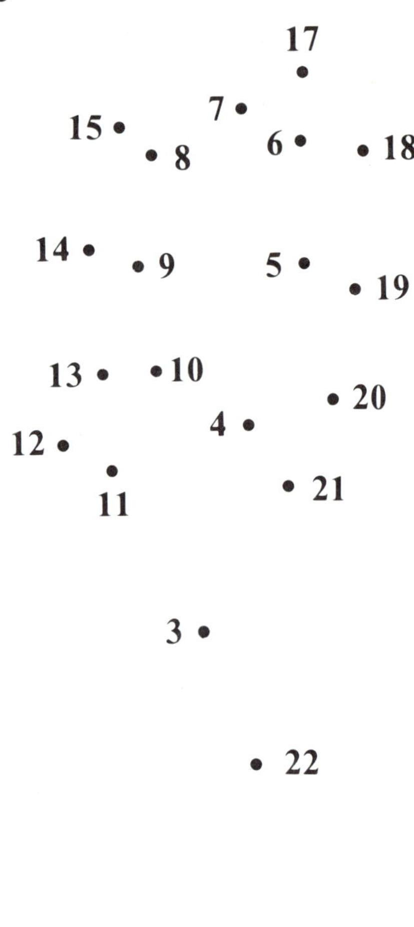

Taking Care of Other People

How do we continue the loving example of Jesus today?

Find some pictures in magazines showing how we can help others. Cut out the pictures and paste them on this page.

Friends of Jesus

Color the pictures of Jesus, Mary, and their friends on the next page.

Cut out the pictures and use them as finger-puppets. Use them to tell a story you know about the life of Jesus.

Make a Holy Week booklet.

Cut out the booklet on the solid lines. Fold it on the
dotted lines. Draw and color a picture on each page
of the booklet. Then unfold the booklet and draw
an Easter picture on the inside.

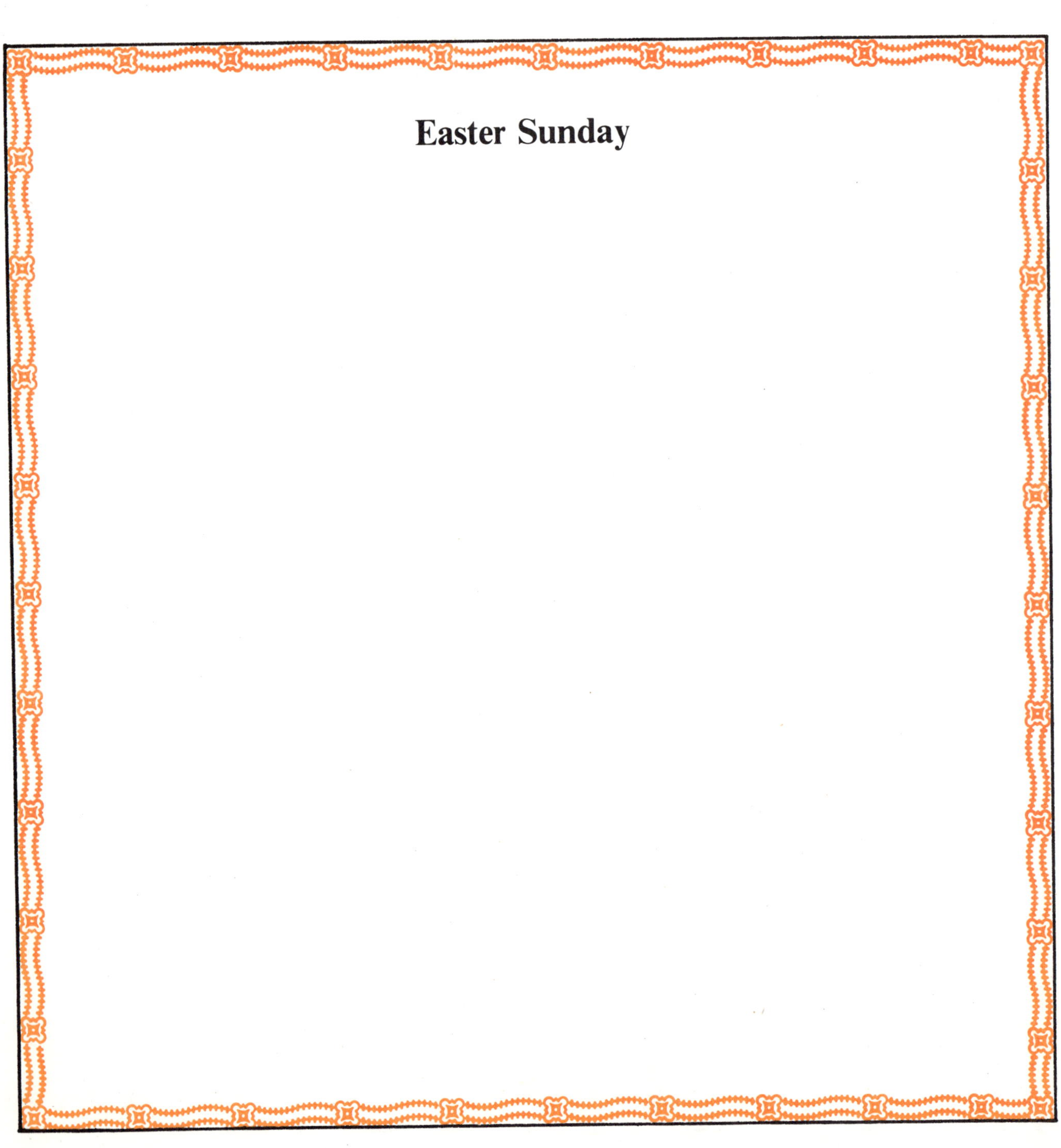

Easter Sunday

The Mass

Color these pictures of a priest celebrating the Mass.

Liturgy of the Word

Liturgy of the Eucharist

My response to God's Word

My response to Jesus in the Eucharist

Happy Halloween!

Here I am in my Halloween costume.

Here I am, happy to be me.

Happy Thanksgiving Day!

Here is a "horn of plenty." Fill it with pictures of the "gifts" you are thankful for. Color the whole picture.

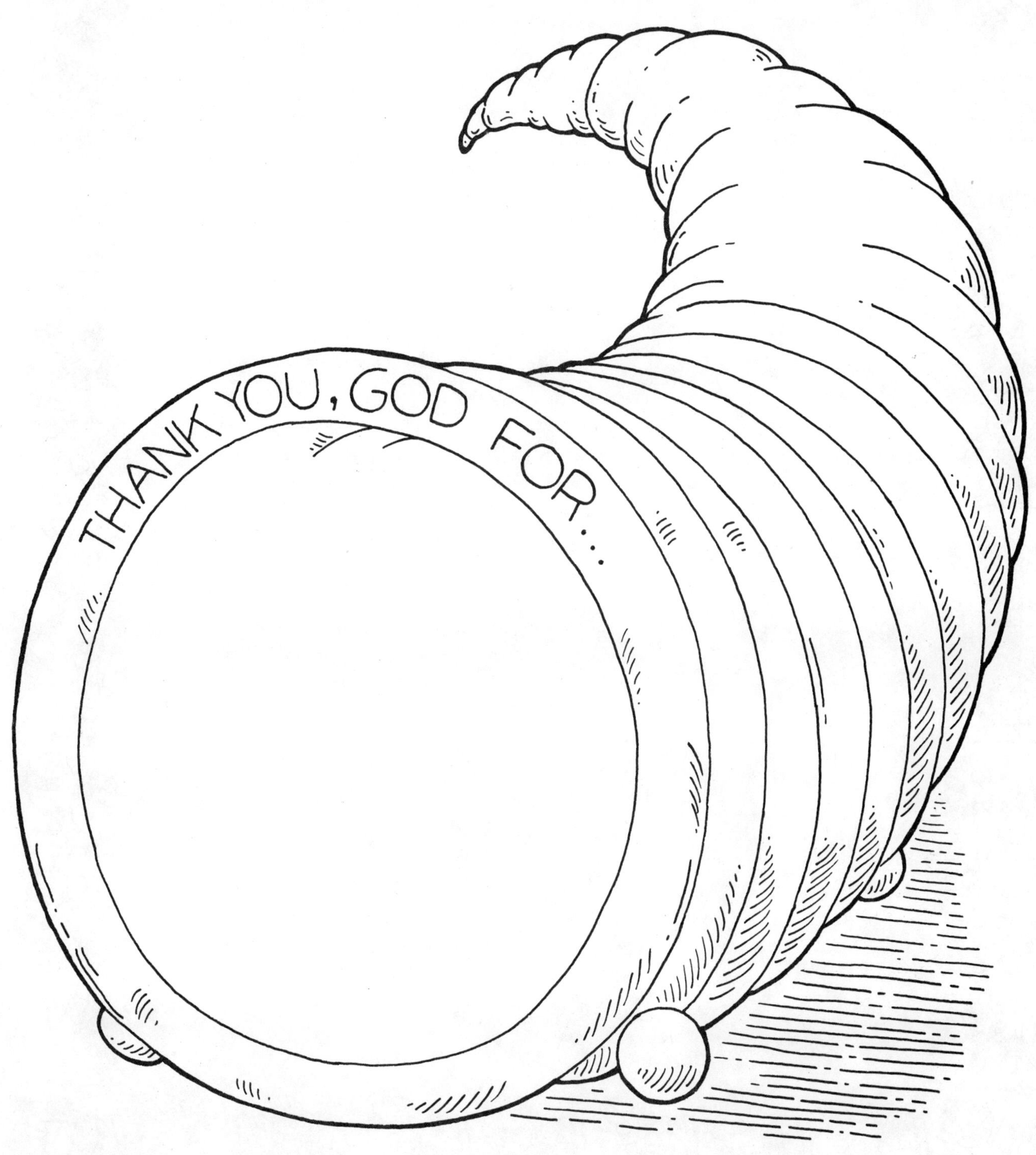

Paste or draw pictures of other things you are
thankful for here.

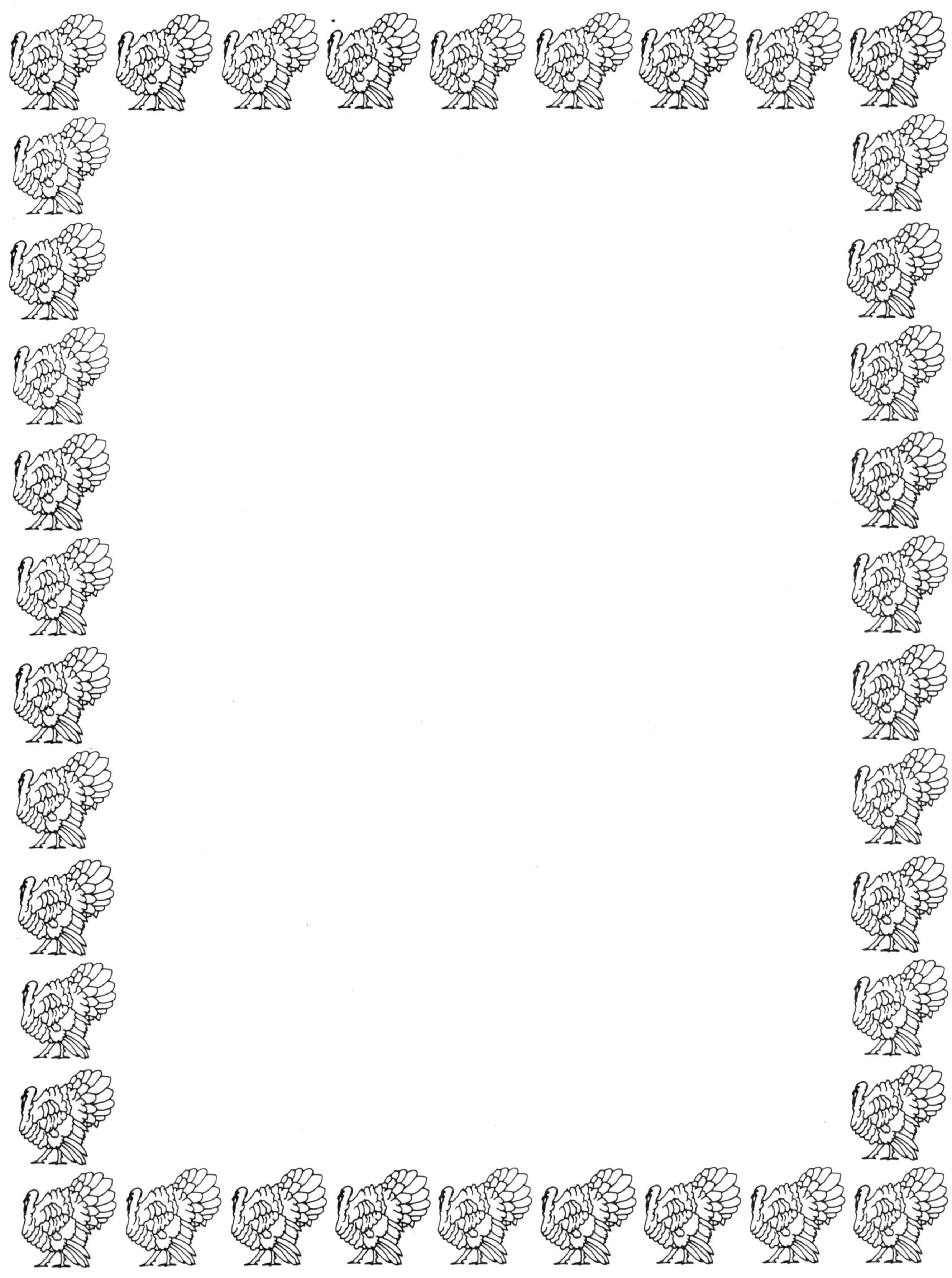

My Advent Calendar

Draw a picture of something you have done each
day to prepare for the birthday of Jesus.

Come, Lord Jesus!

Christmas

Color these pictures. Cut out the pictures. Paste or
tape them into cone-figures. Use them to tell the
story of the birth of Jesus.

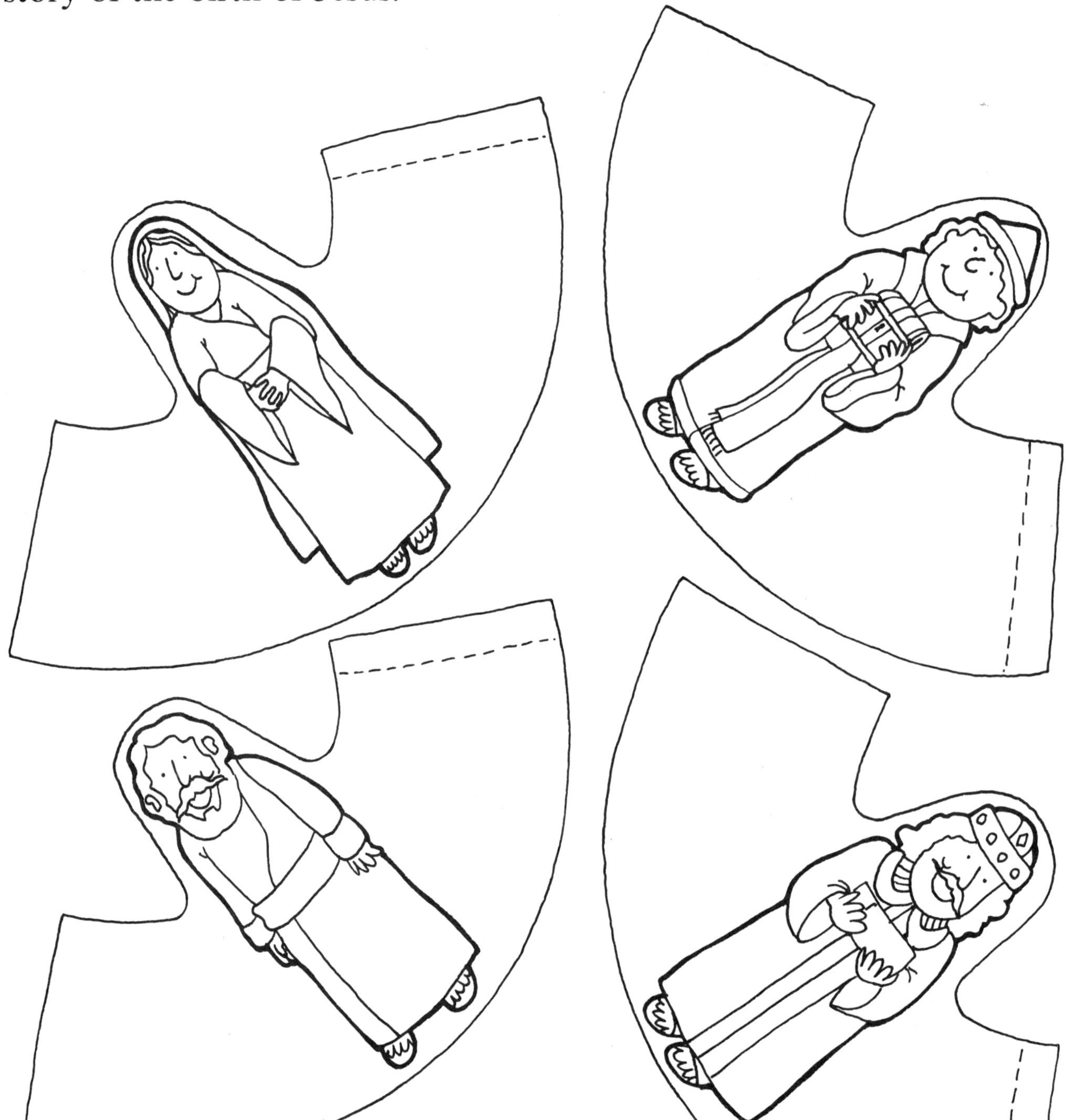

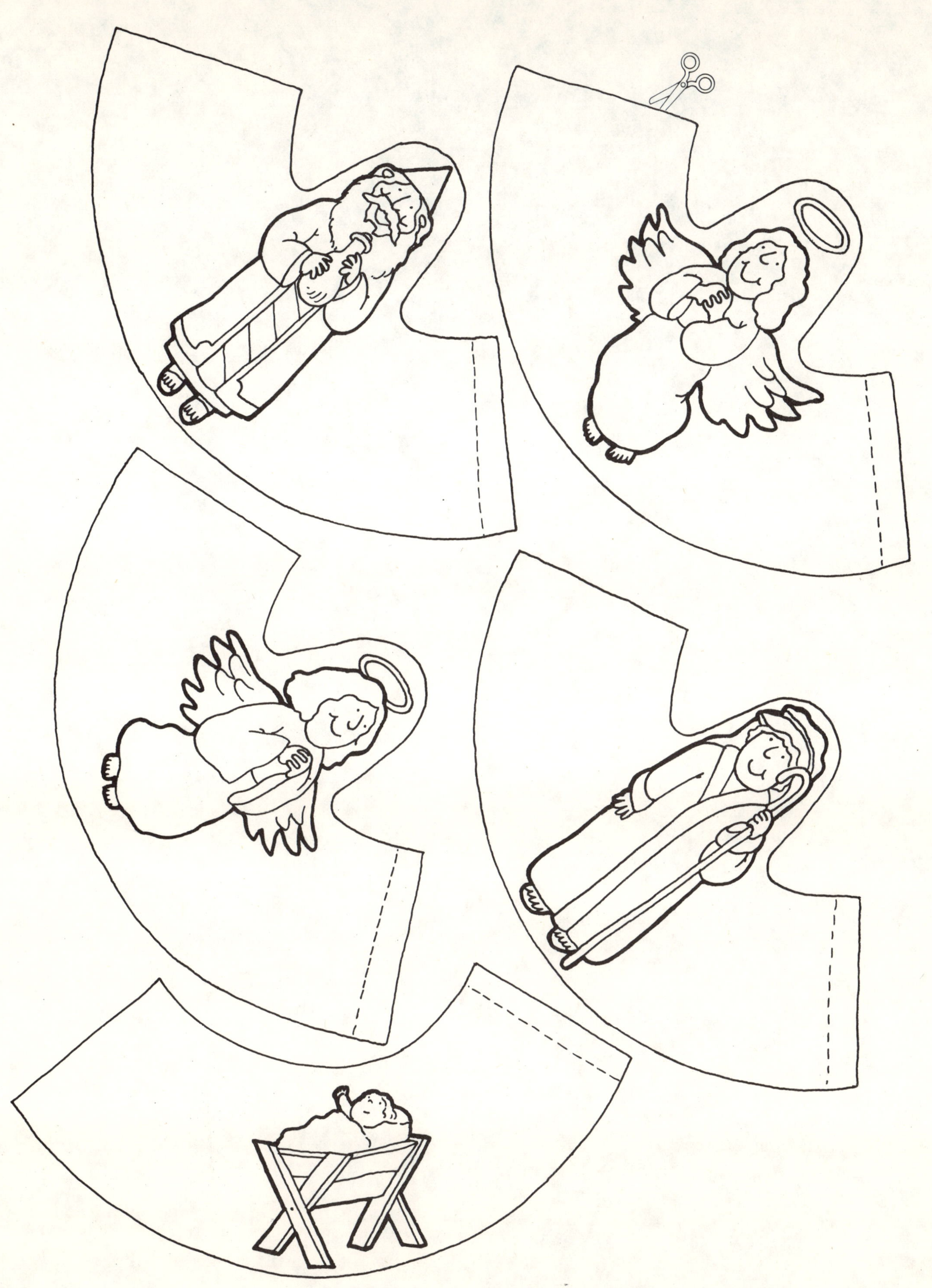

Telling the Story of Christmas

Draw your own story of Jesus' birth.

Draw or paste pictures of other things here that
remind you of new life.

Pentecost

Write in the names of people who have helped you to know God better. Add more balloons, and color them all.